# THE CHANGING

# Eynsham

## BOOK TWO

## Martin J. Harris

Robert Boyd
PUBLICATIONS

Published by
*Robert Boyd Publications*
260 Colwell Drive
Witney, Oxfordshire OX8 7LW

First published 1998

Copyright © Martin J. Harris and
*Robert Boyd Publications*

ISBN: 1 899536 29 9

OTHER TITLES IN THE *CHANGING FACES* SERIES

Banbury: Book One
Bicester: Book One
Bladon with Church Hanborough and
   Long Hanborough
Botley and North Hinksey
Cowley
Cowley: Book Two
Cowley Works: Book One
Cumnor and Appleton with Farmoor
   and Eaton
St Clements and East Oxford:
   Book One
St Clements and East Oxford:
   Book Two
Eynsham: Book One
Headington: Book One
Headington: Book Two
Jericho: Book One
Littlemore and Sandford
Marston: Book One
Marston: Book Two
North Oxford: Book One
North Oxford: Book Two

Oxford City Centre: Book One
South Oxford: Book One
Summertown and Cutteslowe
St Ebbes and St Thomas: Book One
St Ebbes and St Thomas: Book Two
West Oxford
Witney: Book One
Wolvercote with Wytham and Godstow
Woodstock: Book One
Woodstock: Book Two

FORTHCOMING
Abingdon
Banbury: Book Two
Bicester: Book Two
Chipping Norton
Cowley: Book Three
Faringdon and District
Grimsbury
Jericho: Book Two
Kennington
Thame
Yarnton and Begbroke with Cassington

Printed and bound in Great Britain at The Alden Press, Oxford

# Contents

## Cover Illustrations

Front:    Eynsham character Bill Allsworth (1914–1998), Eynsham's 'Starter Upper' at the Eynsham Carnival on 3 July 1976. (Photograph taken by Harry Russell.) This book is a tribute to Bill and all the well-loved Eynsham people who are sadly no longer with us. Bill knew before he died that he would be on the front cover of this book.

Back:    A picture from the carnival 22 years later on 4 July 1998. Left to right: Ron Robinson (Carnival Chairman), Peter Ackling (the new Starter Upper) and Dr Charles Caine who opened this event. The Carnival Queen and her attendants are in the vehicle behind.

# Acknowledgements

I would like to thank the following people who have so kindly lent photographs (and even old negatives!) to me and told me much information about Eynsham: the late Bill Allsworth, Brian Atkins, Ron Axtell, Sarah and Sylvia Ayers, Clara and the late Reg Bloyce, Beryl Buckingham, Jean Buttrick (née Sawyer), Sylvia and Lawrence Chambers, Polly Clifton, Diane and Brian Cox, Julie and Alan Dagg and their delightful children James, Charlotte and Olivia, Vera Davies, Hilda Deville (sister of Bill Allsworth), Jack Douglas, Elsie Floyd, Gladys and Ron Garner, Shirley Gibbons, Stanley and Joan Green, Andy Gwilliam, Ann Haines, Cyril and Rosina Hale, Francis and E Margaret Harris, Mervyn Harris, Michael and Janet Harris, Tom, Alec and Lynn Harris, the late Temperance Hawtin, Barbara and John Horrabin, Aubrey nd Joan Howard, Michael and Jenny Howard, Maureen James, Jeremy's (Oxford Stamp Centre), Carol McNamara, Madame Tussauds (Undine Concannon, Archivist), Andy and Phillis Pimm, Blake Pullen, Bill and Joan Quainton, Joyce Reeves, Sylvia and Tom Richards, Harry and Anne Russell, Mrs R Stevenson, Gerry Thomas, Arthur Titherington (professional photographer at Church Green, Witney), Maurice and Sheila Tree, Bob and Vi Warren, Joan Weedon, Phil Whittaker, Rita Wooldridge.

John Chipperfield and the *Oxford Mail* (Oxford and County Newspapers) deserve a special mention for their permission to use photographs from their archives and the help they have given me.

May I also thank those who have helped with details and encouragement: Barbara Allen, Vince Allen, Geoff Batts, Christopher Betterton, Len and Hebe Betterton, Ken and Elsie Butler, Alec Chalmers, Maureen Clapcott (née Morgan), David Davies, Dot Dormer, Eynsham History Group, Cate Foster, Ron and Connie Gardner, John Harris, June Harris, Ken Harris, Beryl Hastings, Dr and Mrs Bryan Hyde, Sandra Jones and all at the Day Centre, Tracy Kirk, Maureen McCreadie, Dennis and Edna Mason, Karen Mills, Dr Max Peterson and Partners, Moyra Philcox, Kevin Pimm, Phil Pratley, Donald and Pamela Richards, Helen Russell, Robin Saunders, Jack Seeney, Dr and Mrs John Simpson, Josie Smith, Ted Whelan, Leigh Winder, Doug Wixey, Anne Wrapson, Fred and Lilian Wright. Thanks also to BBC Radio 4's *The Archers*, Geoff Parkinson for his help with the layout of the book, and Bob and Pauline Boyd for making it all possible.

A big thank you to any others whose names have been inadvertently omitted and I apologise for any unintentional errors and misleading information that are subsequently discovered.

**A note regarding the quality of the photographs.** Please note that the quality of the photographs included in this book will vary but where the photograph is of a poor standard it has been included for historical reasons or to make a valid point. I hope that this will not effect the enjoyment of the book.

# Amendments to Book 1

Since the publication of the Changing Faces of Eynsham Book 1, many people have kindly come forward with further information and corrections. Some of this information is detailed below. Page numbers refer to those in Book 1.

| Page | |
|---|---|
| 5–7 | The aerial view photograph was taken a few years earlier than 1965 due to the fewer number of houses seen in Back Lane. |
| 29, 60 | The inn was the Maltster and Shovel sometimes called the Malt Shovel. |
| 34 | The procession was in Witney Road. |
| 37 | The toll collector in the picture was Harry (not John) Floyd. |
| 51 | Hockey team: the 1st lady in the middle row was Iris Day (not Woods). |
| 52 | The 1980 Eynsham Morris photo should have listed the people: Back semicircle, left to right: Stan Launchbury, Ian Green, Duncan Briggs (hidden), Dave Townsend, Robin Saunders, Mike Simpson, Robin Mitchell, Bob King, Derek Malin, Ken Sheffield, Dennis Green. Front row (all in suits except Keith Green): Phil Lambourne, Keith Green, Bert Russell, Ernest May. |
| 53 | The man on the big base drum was Henry 'Blower' Russell (born 1846). He was a mill hand at a grain mill on the corner of Abbey Street and Swan Street (which in recent years has been St Winifred's). His wife Mary had 10 children and descendants in Eynsham include members of the Batts, Pimm, Pratley and Russell families. |
| 57 | The Red Lion picture of 1980 had Nicola Saunders on the far right (not her sister Tricia). |
| 62 | The Electrical Sales and Services shop in Acre End Street was started jointly by Vic Allen and Ron Gardner. Ron's son now runs Algar Electric Motors with the help of his relatives and invaluable employees. |
| 63 | Bill Sawyer died in 1994. His wife Vera died in 1989. |
| 69 | In the 1940s class: Alan (not George) Roberts, Judy Brewer (not Quainton). |
| 85 | Eynsham Fire Brigade should be standing, left to right: –, –, –, Ron Harris, Perce Newport, Arthur Belcher, Gordy Evans, Alan Pratley, Bert Evans, –, Bill Robbins. Sitting: Chubby Green, –, –, George Pimm, –, Harold Dixey. Those in the photo below are Alan Pratley (front) and George Green (rear). |
| 87 | The two ladies on the far left of the upper photograph are Elsie Evans with daughter Valerie and Alice Batts with son Geoffrey. It was taken in the back garden of Greywall Cottage, Acre End Street. |
| 91 | The scouts started the carnival and the British Legion helped out in the 1946 carnival (see later in this book for more information). |
| 92 | The lady on the podium was Miss Tessie O'Shea performing on Hanborough playing field in 1952. |
| 95 | In the second photograph Mrs Win Roberts is the third lady down from Harvey Hill. |
| 96 | Many have spotted themselves in this photograph including Jenny Howard (in the ring) and Gary Walker. The lady in the wheelchair was Pam Richard's aunt. |

# Roads to and from Eynsham

Just over the toll bridge can be seen the tall chimney of the sugar beet factory which the author's father walked through in the 1930s when it had been knocked to the ground.

Mrs Josephine Allen (left) and Mrs Louie Treadwell (right) in the mid-1930s during the building of the road that is now the A40 between Eynsham and Oxford.

The turning into Witney Road in the 1960s when travellers between Witney and Botley could not by-pass Eynsham.

## PRIVATE RESIDENTS

Alcock Ralph, The Grange
Anderson George, The Bungalow
Bedford Major-Gen. Sir Walter Geo. Augustus K.C.M.G., C.B. The Holt
Bedford Wm, Orlebar R.N. The Holt
Blake Arthur, Merton, Acre End st
Braithwaite Robert, Laurel cottage
Bricknell Rev. William Nash M.A. (vicar), Mill street
Brooke Miss, The Hermitage, Mill st
Burgin Mrs. Leigh view, Station road
Cantell Mrs. Newland st
Cruickshank Robert Watson M.B., C.M. The Shrubbery, High street
Greatrex Mrs. The Square
Hinks Mrs Blankstone
Irvine Mrs. The Lodge
Oakeley Major Edward Francis J.P. The Gables
Preston William, Queen street
Schmidt Mrs. Chesneys, Newland st
Shillingford Mrs. Acre End street
Smallhorn Mrs. Willow bank, High st
Stevens Mrs. Hy. White ho. Mill st
Swann Mrs. Redthorne house, Mill st
Tindal Jas. The Haven, Newland st
Traill Edmund Bernard, Newland ho
Wastie Miss, Mill street

## COMMERCIAL

Early closing day, Wed 1 p.m.
Applegate Edith (Miss), draper, The Square
Bampton & Eynsham Gas Works (T. F. Ennis, proprietor), Gas lane
Banting William (exors. of), farmers, Acre Hall farm
Banting William, farmer, Mill st
Barclays Bank Ltd. (sub-branch) (open fri. 1 to 4 p.m.); draw on head office, London EC
Beauchamp J. & Sons, grocers & builders, Acre End street
Bennett Edward,shopkpr. Acre End st
Bennett James, basket maker, Chapel yard, Newland street
Biggers John K. baker, High street
Bird Fdk. Geo. Dairyman, Newland st
Blake & Co. mineral water manufacturers, Mill street
Blake Harry, farmer, Merton
Blake Ralph Prior, farmer, The Elms, High street

Buckingham George, calf dealer, Acre End street
Buckingham Robert, Railway inn, Acre End street
Buckingham Samuel, fishmonger, Acre End street
Burden John, blacksmith, Newland st
Calcutt Charles Edward, boot repairer, The Square
Capel Arthur Edward, Newland inn, Newland street
Charles Michael Thomas, fruit growr, Fruitlands
Cruickshank Robert Watson M.B., C.M. Aberd. Surgeon, medical officer & public vaccinator Eynsham district, Witney union & certifying factory surgeon, High street
Dance Albt. Edwd. Shopkpr. Mill st
Dean Thos. Jas. Farmer, Twelve Acres
Fire Engine Station (John Geo. Pimm, captain), High street
Foster -, Red Lion P.H. The Square
Freeman Ernest James, insurance agent, High street
Gardner William James, Queen's Head P.H. Queen street
Gibbons Edwd.Jas.Grocer,Lombard st
Goodwin Henry, motor car proprietor, Newland street
Graham Ernest, motor engineer, 1 Lombard street
Grant Henry William, White Hart P.H. Newland street
Green Bernard Geo. builder, High st
Green Frederick, farmer, City farm
Hall Thos.baker & draper,Acre End st
Harper Percival, farmer & hay & straw merchant, Victoria House fm
Harris Lewis, tailor, 2 Jubilee terrace, High st
Harris Rowland, blacksmith, High st
Hathaway Annie (Miss), midwife, Abbey street
Hathaway John, chimney sweeper, Newland street
Hedges John, butcher, Lombard st
Higgins John, farmer, Bowles farm
Howe Alfred William, drug stores, & Post office, Acre End street
Jennings George Pilchard, Jolly Sportsman P.H. Lombard street

Juggins John, Talbot P.H. Oxford rd
Kirtland Albert Edward, market gardener, Queen street
Lambourne Albert, carrier, Queen st
Pimm Frank, parish clerk, The Square
Pimm John George, grocer, High st
Preston Harry Doyley, frmr. Old frm
Quainton Cyril Thos.Saddler,1 Mill st
Rhodes Thomas, Swan hotel, Acre End street
Rowland Albert, farmer, Mill street
Saunder Philip Edwin, farmer, Abbey farm
Sawyer & Sons, grocers, Newland st
Shankland G. A. Limited, bedding manufacturers, Grange mills &glue &c. manufacturers, Eynsham mills
Stanfield Janet (Mrs.), deputy registrar of births & deaths for Eynsham sub-district, Witney union, Newland street
Stanfield John Henry, relieving & vaccination officer & registrar of births & deaths for Eynsham sub-district of Witney union & school attendance officer, Newland street
State Hannah (Mrs.), beer retailer, Mill street
Stevens William J. grocer, High st
Tindal James, assistant overseer & clerk to the Parish Council, Newland street
Tinson Harry, carrier, High street
Treadwell Jn. Jas. Farmer, Queen st
Wall Lionel, rope ma. Acre End st
Wastie Frederick William, nursery man, High street & Queen street
Whitlock Hy. Baker, Mill street
Wilkins fredk, cycle dlr. Acre End st
Woodbridge Hy. Star inn, Witney rd

## OTHERS

Hall Ernest, constable, Station rd
Faulks Charles, railway station master
Jepson May (Miss), mistress,Station rd, elementary school (infants)
Trethewey Mr John Thomas & Mrs Fanny, school master/mistress, Witney rd, elementary school (boys & girls)

Extracts from the Eynsham section of *Kelly's Directory of Oxfordshire 1920* (courtesy of Reed Information Service) giving details of some, but by no means all, of the Eynsham inhabitants.

# Introduction

Following the success of Book 1 (which has raised over £1,100 for the British Diabetic Association) many people have kindly lent me further Eynsham photographs of the past. It has been difficult to decide which photos to include and some wonderful unpublished pictures will no doubt appear in future publications. There is still much of Eynsham's history to cover and the Eynsham History Group are still keen to hear of any further memories and pictures that people come across.

As well as covering areas of Eynsham not fully covered in Book 1, I have also included sections on the wars, weddings and a look at some of the people behind the Eynsham Carnival over the years. For further details on all aspects of Eynsham please see the *Eynsham Record,* the annual journal published by the Eynsham History Group and edited by Dr Brian Atkins.

All profits that I make from this book will this time go to the Eynsham and Long Hanborough Medical Care Group (registered charity No. 1054256) so a big thank you for helping this charity which will benefit the community in the Eynsham and Long Hanborough area.

On a personal note I would like to say how much enjoyment I have had meeting people from all ages who have told interesting stories about themselves, their families and friends.

A lady who was researching Eynsham's history a few decades before me was Moyra Philcox. If the technology had been available in the 1950s, she would, at that time, have been the author of a book like this. Although Miss Philcox was years ahead of her time, for me she has continued to be a great source of help, always willing to investigate my queries.

I must also say how grateful I am to those who inspired me to have an interest in local history. My history teacher at school, Jill Hibberd (and a former work colleague of Eynsham resident Martin Ford), taught me with unforgettable enthusiasm. Local historian John Hanson and *Eynsham Record* editor Brian Atkins also encouraged me to write down my historical findings.

Finally, my father Francis Harris's fascinating recollections of family memories set me on the trail of family and local history which has continued to this day.

Martin J Harris
Chairman, Eynsham History Group
*October 1998*

# *Around Eynsham*

**High Street shops near the Square**

Ernest Mumford's Hairdresser and Newsagent shop was originally adjoining the Red Lion in the Square. The above photograph was taken prior to the construction in about 1936 of the mock Tudor frontage of the garage in High Street (a popular design in the 1930s). In the later photograph below, Mumford's had moved over the road to the shop which had previously been run by Joseph Culverwell and his wife Annie. Since then, this building has been a newsagent's for the Price family, Mr and Mrs Nichols and the chain Martin.

Adverts from a 1929 Eynsham Parish Magazine which includes, on the top right, Ernest Mumford's business.

During the early part of the 20th century, the building seen in the photograph on the left, which is now a garage on the High Street heading east from the Square, was the site of a blacksmith's run by Rowland Harris, (father of Fred 'butcher' Harris). The frontage was put up by the Bolton brothers, Harry and Charlie ('Skinny') who at that time ran a garage there.

Rowland Harris

The building adjoining the garage is shown here in 1946.

At the turn of the century the Evenlode DIY shop was the site of saddler and harness maker James Davey's business. At one time it had even been part of Gibbons' brewery. The Biggers family took it over as a grocer's before letting it to Ted Bennett in 1932 who kept it as a sweet and tobacco shop.

Following Blake Pullen's marriage to his first wife Veronica Bennett in 1946 he ran the shop as a grocer's until 1968. He then changed it to a DIY shop which Robin Saunders has run since 1975. Joyce Seeney, who came to work for Blake has continued helping out Robin.

Blake Pullen in 1998.

A view of the inside of the shop in the 1950s.

## Lord's Row, Lord's Farm and Miss Foote

This row of cottages, known as Lord's Row, and the adjoining Lord's Farm on the Queen Street/Oxford Road corner were named after James Lord, the probable mason of the toll bridge, who in 1800 was living here. The right half was built at a later date than the left and after 1800.

In the early part of the century, one of the then four cottages was used as a cycle shop by Frederick Browne (known as Leo Browne). The signboard outside the shop said (variations have been reported):

Here lives the man who'll ne'er refuse
To mend all sorts of inner tubes!
All kinds of cycles he'll repair,
And only charge you what is fair.

He'll mend a puncture in your tyre,
Or let you out a bike on hire.
The lot is good. The work is just,
The profits small so cannot trust.

Browne left Eynsham under police escort in 1910. He returned with William Kennedy on 5 December 1927 in an attempt to rob the Railway Station. Although their aim was to rob the safe, after tying up the railway porter Fred Castle, they only managed to steal a typewriter, some tobacco and parcels.

Fred was extremely fortunate as they were on the run from murdering an Essex policeman, PC Gutteridge, in September of that year. The policeman had been shot through the eyes. A taxi was also stolen from Herbert Berrie in Jericho. Berrie's grandson, Michael Baston, has lived in nearby Farmoor for many years. Both Browne and Kennedy were executed for their crimes. Their waxworks, as shown below, were on display in Madame Tussauds' Chamber of Horrors in London from 1928 to 1965.

Browne (left) and Kennedy. (Courtesy Madame Tussauds)

When Miss Margaret Foote, seen here in her garden, came to live at Lord's Farm in 1952 it was called Wadhurst and so she promptly restored the traditional name. She also had Lord's Row renovated with the four cottages converted into two, the work being completed in March 1960. Previously, each cottage had consisted of just one room downstairs and one upstairs with a very small landing bedroom (except one cottage which lacked even this).

Following Miss Foote's death in 1983, the property was left to the Oxford Preservation Trust.

Miss Foote's Good News van was a former horse-drawn bread van previously owned by the Biggers family. It contained bibles and Christian writings and was regularly used on carnival days.

## Queen Street

Queen Street from the south end looking north in the 1920s. Note the washing line behind the stone wall on the left. Just out of view on the left were stables and a yard attached to Hill House.

Phillis Harris in the yard attached to Hill House in the early 1930s.

In this set of photographs it can be seen how the Hill House yard, sometimes referred to as Trap Alley, looked in the 1930s with a car and donkey, in the Spring of 1966 looking derelict, and being renovated and converted into houses in 1967.

## Elm Cottages

Elm Cottages off Queen's Lane.

In the immediate post-war/early 1950s the residents were:

| West | | | | | | East |
|---|---|---|---|---|---|---|
| 1 | 2 | 3 | 4 | 5 | 6 | 7 |
| Freda and Tommy Boggs | Mr and Mrs Harris | Lena and Selina Smith | Doris and Jack Pinker | Ned and Fanny Harris | Ben Ayers Sybil & Ted Ayers | Rose and Perce Grant |

The Pinkers' children included Evelyn (now Smith), Dorsey, Reg, Peter and John. Ned and Fanny Harris' daughter Freda married Ron Gregory at Eynsham in 1945. The Grants' daughter Peggy married Urbin and Temperance Hawtin's son Ken. In the thatched cottage to the right of the Grants lived Mrs Edwards and her two Pekinese dogs. In 1954 Ted Whelan and his wife, Hilda, moved into the cottage.

Ted Whelan (right) taken in 1996 talking to Dr Kate Ferrier's father Alec Chalmers.
Hilda Whelan had some of her poetry published in the Witney Gazette as well as in a
book called "My Song."

Ted Ayers with his wife Sylvia and
daughter Sarah on the day of her
christening in 1950. Sylvia Ayers
(née Jordan) came to Eynsham in
1920 from Dentford near
Hungerford to 12 Acre Farm (the
Nunnery). The couple married in
1937. Ted Ayers (who died in 1960)
worked for the Pimms and in the
mid to late 1950s worked for
builder Harvey Hill.

Ted's father was Benjamin Ayers (shown here in both photographs) who married Sarah Douglas at Eynsham in 1907. In the picture on the left, the pathway heading north is now Newland Close (Newland Cottage in Newland Street can just be seen in the distance). The second photo, taken in 1955, shows Benjamin at the back of Queen's Lane.

## Barclays Bank

Barclays Bank has had various sites in Eynsham over the years. Here it is shown during the inter-war years on the corner of High Street and Lombard Street next to where Stevens' bakery was. This site is said to have once been a Court House for Eynsham. The corner was a popular place for people to stand and have a chat with others or just watch the activity going on around the area. There was also a bell outside. In recent years the site has been a Co-op food shop.

Before moving to a converted barn in Mill Street, Barclays had banking facilities in Acre End Street. In the early 1950s, Dennis Mason would provide a banking service on a Tuesday morning in the chemist's shop in Acre End Street. Others recall Blake's Grange Mill in Acre End Street also being used.

In 1974 Dennis was sub-manager of the Mill Street bank and his wife Edna made an iced fruit cake in the shape of the bank to mark the first anniversary of the bank being a full branch rather than just a sub-branch. The Eynsham branch closed in the early 1990s with the cashpoint machine moved in the mid-90s to the shopping area in Spareacre Lane. (Oxford and County Newspapers)

**Station Road**

Shown above in a picture from the early 20th century is where, until the 1970s, the railway crossed Station Road. In later years, before the Oxford Instruments building was built, 'Donkey Joe' Smith kept part of the nearby land as an allotment and let some of his animals graze there.

**Acre End Street**

Acre End Street taken prior to World War I.

The same road further into the centre showing celebrations for King George V's coronation on 22 June 1911. (Jeremy's Postcards)

Celebratory events, held the following day, included a meal for the elderly and a procession of about 400 children through the village, finishing at Litchfield (courtesy of Mrs Mary Saunder) where they were given tea and a coronation mug. After sporting events for all ages, there was dancing in the evening to the Kennington Prize Band.

**The Witney Roads**

Members of the Harris family in Witney Road in the late 1920s/early 1930s with the Star Inn in the background. Left to right: Ernest 'Codgell' Harris, his sister-in-law Miriam 'Midge' Harris, her son Francis, Codgell's wife Mildred, Midge's daughter Jean.

The nickname of Codgell arose when, as a toddler playing in the stable of the family home, someone commented, 'Oh mind that little Codgell.'

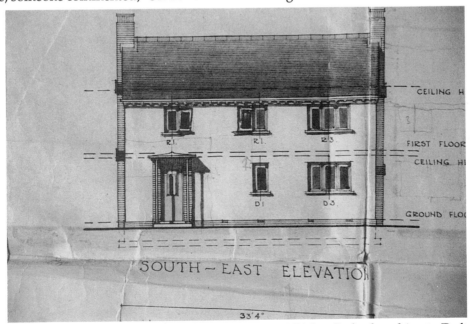

The house plan of 4 (Old) Witney Road drawn in 1954 by Oxford architects Daft and Cave and built by the Hill brothers.

The original All Views, shown here in the 1930s, was built after the 1914–18 War by poultry farmer Mr Jimmy White and his wife Rose who came from Reading and whose daughter was Mrs Butler of the Jolly Sportsman. It was constructed of brick under an asbestos slated roof in over seven acres of land.

It has been said it was named All Views because it had large windows all round.

In 1934 Tommy Harris and his bride Rose Neville moved into the house which had been purchased by Tommy's brother-in-law Reg Bloyce. The Whites left Eynsham to live their retirement in the Reading area. Shortly afterwards, Tommy's parents moved in next door to Moorland, a name the Harris family gave to it when they purchased it. The previous and original owners since it was built in about 1922–23 were Mr O'Connor, a retired Irish schoolmaster, who lived there with his wife and daughter.

After his parents' deaths, Tommy Harris bought and moved next door to Moorland and his sister Gertie Hale and her family moved into All Views. In 1983, following Gertie's death aged 79, the property was sold to Gerry Thomas who had to demolish the building and build a new All Views. Gerry has run the property as a farm shop, nursery and guest house.

All Views in 1983 showing the flat roofed extension at the rear.

The property just prior to demolition.

The demolition of All Views captured on film by Lynn Bond (later Harris).

All Views in 1998.

The rear of Moorland in 1936. Note the outside copper which was used for heating water.

**Changes in the 1960s and 1970s**

A view from 1972 of the water tower in Mill Street being demolished by Mr Archie Brown. Built in 1903, water was pumped to the tower from a well in a field adjoining Cassington Road. It had been standing idle since 1967 when the Oxfordshire and District Water Board was formed. The huge metal tank on top of the brick tower was cut into pieces and lowered to the ground. (Oxford and County Newspapers)

A view looking west from near the Back Lane/Evans Road junction showing Pye's development in Shakespeare Road and the entrance to Falstaff Close.

Above: the site of Wytham Close, off Wytham View, just before its development, showing archaeologists carrying out an exploratory dig.

John Lopes Road in 1967 showing a half-finished pavement. John Lopes was the Roman Catholic priest.

## Other Eynsham streets and roads

The antiques shop run by Harry Lamb in Newland Street which adjoined Redthorne House. Next to the antiques shop was Polish war refugee Johnny Gardias' cobbler's shop. Johnny married Eynsham's Dorsey Pinker. The lady walking up the street is Mrs Dormer from Queen Street.

Back Lane as it looked before houses were built there.

Eynsham Lock

The present day Eynsham Lock, as shown in its early years above, was opened in 1928. Although in the parish of Cumnor, the lock keepers have usually had much to do with Eynsham life. In the 1930s the Long family resided in the house.
In 1969 Brian and Jean West left the lock to go to Sonning and were replaced by Brian and Maureen McCreadie who had previously been at Marlow. Bill has been a great supporter of Eynsham Social Club and Maureen has for quite a few years been the editor of the parish newsletter the Eynsham Roundabout.

Maureen McCreadie serving teas in her garden in 1998.

# Church Life and Weddings

The Revd Stuart Blanch and the Baptist minister, the Revd Richard Hamper, dressed as Benedictine monks at the 1955 Eynsham Carnival with Miss Foote's Bible cart.

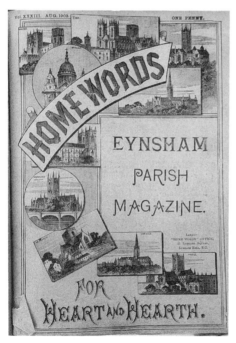

The front pages of Eynsham Parish Magazine from 1903 and 1936.

Rogation parades through Eynsham in the late 1940s or early 1950s with the Rev David Peck. Amongst those in the photograph above in Acre End Street are Cecil Calcutt (Special Constable) with Churchwardens Mr Belcher and Mr Bernard Green behind. In the photograph below, on the A40, Mr Belcher and Bevan Pimm are behind the vicar and John Pimm is holding the banner.

| | | 04 | 07 | | 11 | | 14 15 | | S | | | 24 25 | | | |
|---|---|---|---|---|---|---|---|---|---|---|---|---|---|---|---|
| | 02 | | 05 | 08 | | 12 | 16 | 17 | | 19 | 21 22 | 26 28 | | 30 | 32 |
| 01 | 03 | 06 | 09 | 10 | 13 | | | 18 | | 20 | 23 | 27 | 29 | 31 | |

The Church Choir outside St Leonard's in the 1970s on one of Stuart Blanch's return visits.
01 John Burden, 02 Pamela Richards, 03 Linda Ayres?, 04 Joan Green, 05 Alan Garner, 0€
Maxine Kimber, 07 Colin Hopcroft, 08 Freda Johnson, 09 Calcutt twin★, 10 Michael White
11 Noel Lindsay, 12 —, 13 Calcutt twin★, 14 —, 15 —, 16 Jane Oliver, 17 Lucy Richards, 1£
Judith Butler-Miles, S Stuart Blanch, 19 Christine Hopcroft, 20 Sue Floyd?, 21 Brend£
Butler-Miles, 22 Joan Calcutt, 23 Martin Richards, 24 George Johnson, 25 Donald Richards
26 Pat Brown, 27 Sandra Hopcroft, 28 —, 29 Mandy Duffield, 30 Albert Hicks, 31 Georgin£
Brown, 32 Stanley Green.
★ Jonathan and Julian Calcutt.

George and Freda Johnson, who lived in Duncan Close, were involved with St Leonard'
Church during the 1970s and 1980s. George was a churchwarden and his wife was PCC
secretary. They left Eynsham in the late 1980s for Norfolk. At their funerals a few years ag«
the Queen's chaplain attended.

t Peter's Roman Catholic Church, as it looked in 1963, showing the so-called temporary' wooden nave adjoined to the stone-built part. The full building was halted y the outbreak of World War II. Work was resumed soon after this photograph was aken. (Oxford and County Newspapers)

Father John Lopes at an event in the Square.

## Weddings

The wedding at St Leonard's of Elsie Mercer to Walter Floyd on 12 October 1935. The bridesmaids and best man outside the church from left to right: Mary Burnard, Ernie 'Slogger' Floyd, Eileen Ayling and Walter's cousin Elsie Bentley (who married Ken Butler).

A picture taken at the Star where the reception was held. Those standing, left to right: Eileen Ayling, her father Bill Killick, Walter Floyd, Ernie Floyd, Elsie Floyd, her mother Clara Mercer. The seated bridesmaids: Elsie Bentley (left) and Mary Burnard (right).

The wedding of Sylvia Howard to Lawrence Chambers at St Peter's on 6 September 1952. Left to right (adults): May and Albert Chambers (groom's parents), Barbara Howard/Grimshaw, Arthur Simister (best man), groom and bride, Aubrey Howard, Arthur and Elsie Howard (bride's parents), Georgina Howard. The young bridesmaids were Rosemary Dixey (left) and Lesley Chambers (right).

The wedding of Janet Timms to butcher Mervyn Harris at St Leonard's on 6 July 1953. Left to right: Mary Timms (Janet's twin sister), groom, bride, Ken Harris (brother), Margaret Timms (sister). They were one of the first couples to be married at Eynsham by Stuart Blanch.

The wedding of Diane Gallagher to Brian Cox at St Peter's in 1962. Left to right: Rober
Goff, Margaret Wilson, Beryl Gallagher, Flo —, Lily Cox, Roy Cox, groom, bride, Bol
Warren, Hilda Gallagher behind Leonard James Ayres, Pat Gallagher, Dolly Samuels
Janet Ayres, Ann Roche, Win Phipps, Lovie Williams, Jenny Grimes, Lil Grimes
Magaret Gallagher, Bill Roche, Violet Warren.

The wedding of Leigh Bolsover to Peter Winder at St Leonard's on 12 March 1966
Peter's widowed father, Eric Winder of Harrogate, Yorkshire, is on the left with Leigh's
parents Yoma and Dr Derrick Bolsover on the right. Peter was then a pilot in the RAF.

## Not a Real Wedding!

In 1972, in an episode of BBC Radio 4's successful show The Archers, Martha Lily (played by Eynsham's Mollie Harris) married woodworker Joby Woodford (George Woolley). The congregation included members of Eynsham's Women's Institute who Mollie had kindly invited to the BBC studios.

| | 23 | | | 24 | 25 | 26 | 27 | 28 | 29 | 30 |
|---|---|---|---|---|---|---|---|---|---|---|
| 14 | 15 | | | 16 | 17 | 18 | 19 | 20 | 21 | 22 |
| | 8 | G | B | 9 | 10 | 11 | 12 | 13 | | |
| | 4 | | | 5 | 6 | | | | | |
| | 1 | | | 2 | 3 | | | | | |

The groom (G) and bride (B) George Woolley and Mollie Harris. 1 Doris Hicks, 2 –, 3 –, 4 June Pettit, 5 Julia Durbin, 6 Elsie Floyd, 7 –, 8 Elsie Evans, 9 Mrs Evans?, 10 Beryl Hastings, 11 Mary Evans, 12 Alice Winterbourne, 13 Mr Brooks, 14 –, 15 –, 16 Joyce Treadwell, 17 Joan Hooper, 18 Joan Howard, 19 Pat Burton, 20 Rosie Peachey, 21 Eva Crawford, 22 Mark Crawford, 23 Mary Douglas?, 24 Jean Alder. Sisters: 25 Rosa Green, 26 Nancy Butler-Miles and 27 Emmie Harbud (née Dixey), 28 –, 29 –, 30 –.

## Whittaker's Weekend

From Friday 3 September 1982 until the following Tuesday, fundraising events took place in Eynsham to raise money for St Leonard's church restoration appeal. As churchwarden Phil Whittaker was greatly involved in its planning it was decided to call the programme 'Whittaker's Weekend.' Following a talk by Mr Brookin on China in the Baptist Hall, the 'Weekend' was launched the following morning in the Square with the Boys' Brigade Band, the Majorettes and the Eynsham Morris. All were catered for with

events such as a jumble sale, whist drive, film shows, a football match, choral evensong and a history exhibition. A clay pigeon shoot took place at City Farm on the Sunday along with sports on the playing field. The extended 'Weekend' was rounded off with concerts in St Leonard's on the Monday and Tuesday evenings.

Phil Whittaker and the vicar Peter Ridley.

The Majorettes, who performed throughout the Saturday and Sunday, were trained by Sarah Ayers, the keep fit instructor.
In the photo, Sarah is on the far left. The dancers that can be seen, from left to right: Jane Gilby, Heidi Barrass, Joanne Barrass, Lyn Collins, Amanda Brain, Sarah Webb, Diane Whitlock. Also out of view are Deborah Massey, Emily Gurney, Lisa Howley and Lynn, –.

Elsie Floyd (with hat) and teacher Anne Price at an exhibition. Elsie was a keen supporter of Whittacker's Weekend. Anne is the longest-serving teacher at the Beech Road Primary School and was there when it first opened.

Sealed knot soldiers are seen here in the vicarage garden.

At 7 p.m. on the Sunday, following music by a brass band, an open air service was held just outside the church. One of the organisers of the weekend, Alec Chalmers, is seen here at the microphone.

# *Football and Boxing*

**Football teams**

Eynsham's Football Club 1937–38. Back row: Eric Barker, Jack Douglas, Peter Blunt, Ronald Butler, Douglas Woolston, Ronald Harling, Wilf Watkins, Mr Titchell (who ran the club). Front row: Harry Green, Bill Quainton, – Franklin, Arthur Buckingham, George Caple, Bert Evans, George Cowie.

A successful team probably from the 1940s. Back row, left to right: –, Jack Green, Les Gwyn, Ken Smith, Cicel Batts, Ern Russell, Boss Perkins. Front row: Len Wiggins, Ern Howard, Bill Perkins, Bill Warner (from Farmoor), Ron Harling.

Eynsham Football Club 1947–48 who won three trophies: Witney and District FA Champions, Fred Ford Memorial Trophy (both for the second year in succession), and the County Junior Shield. Back row, left to right: Leonard Pimm (secretary), Len Gardner (committee), Alex Skene (committee), Tommy G Brooks (chairman), Wilfred Watkins (committee), Bill Perkins (committee), Arthur Brooks (committee), Alan Pratley (treasurer). Middle row: Charles E Philcox (vice-president), Frank 'Jammy' James, Raymond Green, George 'Jock' Campbell, Kenneth Smith, John Mitchell, Reg Treadwell, Aubrey? Green, Herbert Buckingham (president). Front row: Roy Parsloe (trainer), Jock Cochrane, Arthur Buckingham (vice-captain), Cecil Batts (captain), Walter Buckingham, Frank Pimm, Billy Betterton (committee).

About 130 people who were members and friends of the club celebrated their triple success at the annual dinner held at the Institute. All three trophies were on display at the event and entertainment was provided by Reg Froude's Entertainers.

Eynsham Football Club 1951–52, winners of the Witney and District FA Stuart Cup and champions of Witney and District FA Reserve League. Back row, left to right: Frank James (trainer), Mike Brooks (committee), Albert Axtell (committee), Len Pimm (secretary), Reg Hooper (chairman — also father of Mike Hooper), Arthur Brooks (committee), Tommy Brooks (committee). 2nd row: Aubrey Howard, Wilf Bayliss, Aubrey Clifton (who married Polly Treadwell), Maurice Tree, Tony Humphries, Don 'darky' Allen, Frank Pimm, Reg Treadwell, Basil Whelan. Front row: Norman Pratley, Harold Turner, Bertie L Whelan (captain), Walter Buckingham, Mike Hooper.

Eynsham Football Club for the 1960–61 season won the Witney Senior Cup. Standing at the back: John Maskell. Second row, left to right: George Hedges, Marshall Haines (vice captain), Brian Duffield, Don Allen, David Batts. Front row: Georgie Leigh?, Michael Batts, Pat Woolley (captain), David May, Eddy Quainton. (Photo: A Titherington)

## Boxing

Bill Quainton, born 1921, son of the saddler Cyril 'Ducky' Quainton, got into boxing at the early age of eight years. One evening he went along to the infants school in Station Road and for 1d per week was a member of Eynsham's boxing club. Under the guidance of Joe Alford and Harry Wiggins a group of youngsters practised on Tuesday and Thursday evenings and Sunday mornings, usually in a room in pubs like the Railway Inn and the Red Lion. A chalk mark would outline the ring area. Both Bill and other Eynsham people like Harry's son Len Wiggins would fight at tournaments against other amateur boxers in the Oxford area. Hanborough's Arthur Leach also used to come to the club. Each morning except Sunday Bill would start his day at 7.20 a.m. delivering newspapers for Ernie Mumford, returning home at 8.30 for practice on a punchbag which was a bag filled with sawdust hung in his father's shed. The floor above Harris's butcher's shop was also once used by a boxing club.

Bill's under-9 boxing medal.

Bill Quainton as a child in his sporting gear.

Cyril Quainton acquired the nickname Ducky when, as a youngster, he was down by the river watching some lads fishing. Whilst they threatened to throw him in the river if he didn't 'clear off', Cyril slipped in and managed to swim without difficulty. His mother then gave him the nickname Ducky.

# *Pubs and Cafés*

The Jolly Sportsman on the corner of Lombard Street and Acre End Street (then High Street) taken in 1957. It was owned then, as it is now, by Halls. In the 1920s and 1930s Ted and Lilian Butler were the landlords living with their children Ken, Eunice, Ron (who died young) and Eileen. They had previously lived in Reading. (Oxford and County Newspapers)

The Evenlode Hotel was opened in 1936 to cater for the growing motor vehicle traffic travelling along the Witney Road. It used to have petrol pumps at one time operated by World War I veteran Wilfred Watkins. Despite losing a leg in the war he was an excellent cricketer and others would run for him when he was batting for Eynsham's team. There  would also sometimes be an RAC man standing nearby outside the RAC phone box on the corner of the Old Witney Road and the A40.

The inn sign of the New Inn at the south end of Mill Street shown early this century when it was run by Bob Buckingham. Constables the bakers can also be seen here.

The Railway Inn taken in the early 1930s by which time the Buckinghams had established themselves there. The young girl is Bob's granddaughter, Barbara Hill (later Horrabin), standing with Judy the dog. To the right is her uncle Nelson Hill who died in 1934. Interestingly, Charles Yateman moved from being landlord of the Railway Inn to the New Inn in 1871.

The Queen's Head in Queen Street taken in 1935. The gentleman on the road is Frederick Ayres. Mr Jack Thornton became the landlord in 1947 and his family remained there for 27 years before he and his wife retired to Ducklington.

Some of the Queen's Head's regulars and friends in the 1960s. Left to right: Ron Young, Enid Thornton (Jack's wife), Cliff Bennett, Jim Bedding, George Jefferies, Smag Ayres, —, Joan Reeve, Jack Thornton, —.

George Haines' Crossways Café

Rita Harwood (later Truby) standing on the other side of the counter to George Haines and his wife Emily. Their son George can just be seen behind the hatch.

The name 'Crossways' arose because it was near the crossroads where the Hanborough Road was intersected by the Oxford to Witney road. This intersection has since been blocked off with the road to the Hanboroughs north of the A40 moved slightly to the east.

Originally the Haines family had a fish and chip shop at the northern end of Queen Street. The Crossways Café was built in 1955 opposite the furthest north entrance to Wytham View and demolished in 1968 for houses in Hanborough Close.

Crossways Café in 1961. The young girl is George's daughter Maureen.

The Crossways Café demolished.

The site in 1998 showing Marlborough Close.

### The San Remo Café, Witney Road

Harry and Stella Merchant came to Eynsham in 1936/7 from Witney with their two children Sylvia and Ron (younger sister Carol was born in the 1940s). Just after the war started, their house on the Witney road, between the Evenlode and Moorland, was opened as a transport café to assist in the war effort. It was named San Remo after the place in northern Italy.

During the early years, Mollie Harris, who was working for Tarrants shop in Witney, would often deliver supplies to the café such as dried egg and instant potato. At a moment's notice, troops would arrive expecting to be fed. A budding young actress often used to call in when travelling through the area. Her name was Julie Andrews, the very lady who went on to become internationally famous starring in films such as 'The Sound of Music' and 'Mary Poppins' in the 1960s. Stella Merchant was also a talented lady as she had poetry published in the *Witney Gazette.*

Tele: Eynsham 241.

## SAN REMO CAFE'
(Proprietors: H & S. F. MERCHANT )

*Open all day—every day for*
**Breakfasts - Lunches - Teas - Suppers - Snacks**
*at Moderate Charges.*

NORTHERN BY-PASS, EYNSHAM, OXON.

Presented by.......................................................

In the 1970s and 1980s the site was home to a Little Chef which eventually moved over the road near Wastie's garage.

Harry and Stella Merchant.

Ron Merchant who died in 1978 aged 45 and was buried in Eynsham churchyard.

The shop which has been the Pantry in Acre End Street, selling health foods and sandwiches, was once the Gift Shop selling antiques in the late 1950s run by Mrs Stella Merchant after she sold the San Remo café in 1957. This picture shows her daughters Sylvia and Carol outside the property. Stella also had antiques shops in Bladon and Witney.

# *Schools and Schoolchildren*

Eynsham infants in either 1929 or 1930 in the front garden of the school in Station Road. Those identified include in the back row, left to right: −, −, Cliff Russell, −, Gladys Ainsley, −. Middle row: −, Joan Webb, −, − Betterton?, Josie Pimm, Graham Whelan, Veronica Bennett, −, Stanley Green, David Wastie, Freda Harris. Front rows: −, Eileen Butler, Harry 'Jack' Hardwick, Geoffrey Philips, Joan Drewitt, Ruth Pimm,−.

A nativity play at the infants school in the late 20s/early 30s. Back row, left to right: Josie Pimm, Joan Drewitt. 2nd row: Maorie Axtell, Gladys Ainsley, Ernie Ayris, Raymond Floyd, Dora Ashton. Front row: Eileen Butler, Hebe Treadwell, Helen Russell, Gladys Evans.

The Board School in Witney Road as it looked in the early 20th century.

Pupils from that school in 1929/30 with teacher John Farnish. Back row, left to right: −, −, Gladys Whitehall, Lydia Leach, Eunice Butler, Phillis Brooks, −, Bill Perkins. Second row: Elsie Pratley, Pearl Beach, Eva Evans, −, Hilda Allsworth, Doris Mott, Francis Whelan, Dorothy Langford. Third row: Ron Matthews, Ernest Russell, Hubert May, Ron Harling, −, Cyril Ainsley, Reg Quainton, −. Front row: Hilda Wood, −, Doris Walker, Veronica Perrin, Joan Wiggins.

Oxfordshire
Education Committee.

N° 2052

## SCHOOL RECORD.

*Eynsham* _Central School._

This Record has reference to the period from
11 years onwards.

Name in Full *Harry Russell*

Date of Birth *14.6.1920*

Name and Address of Parent or Guardian—
*Mr. Henry Russell*
*6 Spareacre Place, Eynsham*

Date of Admission *25.4.1927*
Date of Leaving *3.8.1934*

Previous Central Schools attended (if any)—

Harry Russell's School Record on leaving aged 14 years. The report, signed by Mr Farnish, commented 'A very intelligent boy. Is thoroughly reliable and so an excellent worker. He is the top boy in the school.' Harry went on to be a popular postman in the Eynsham area.

Harry Russell the postman.

A school photograph from the late 1930s. Back row, left to right: Basil Seeney, –, Dudley Hooper, Ken Harris, Ray Ayres, Ray 'Nobby' Clark, Raymond Titchell, Stuart Simmonds, Albert Axtell, –. Second row: –, Betty Maynard, –, Pat Ayres, –, Pat Evans, Ken Hawtin, Maurice Tree, Maurice Bailey. Third row: Jean Wiggins, Margaret Tibbetts, Joan Hedges, Kathy Spicer, –, Audrey Perrin, Yvonne Pimm. Front row: Gordon Edwards, Leslie Belcher, Don Allen, Murray Burham, Clifford Pimm, Bill? Hammond, Bill Hayward, Des Ashton, John Stevens, Peter Woolley.

A class from 1945/6. Back row, left to right: Alan Long, Hazel Belcher, –, Doreen Grant, Michael Green, Shirley Hanks. Next two standing rows: Nina Woolley, Trevor Green, Alan Fleet, Roy Batts, Myrtle Spicer, Dodie Smith, Rex Pancott, –, Glenys Thomas, Sylvia Booker, Johnny Harris, Dougie Wixey, Yvonne Broadhurst. Front standing row: Myra Pimm, Michael Howard, Margaret Broadhurst, Percy Vaughan, Coral Woodhouse. Next row (sitting): Jean Clark(e), Desmond Newport, Shirley Morgan, Kenneth Harwood, Joy Parker. Front sitting row: Charlie Willis, Michael Pratley, Beryl Bond, David Launchbury, June Drewitt.

An early aerial view of the Beech Road Primary School built in 1967. (Oxford and County Newspapers)

Teachers Mrs Elsie 'Peckham' Lane and Mrs Kay Chapman (wearing glasses) with pupils on their retirement from the primary school in 1973. (Oxford and County Newspapers)

Bartholomew School, as it looked when it was first opened in 1958 by Mr Michae Mason of Eynsham Hall. (Oxford and County Newspapers)

Mr Edwin 'Steve' Stevenson was headmaster from its beginnings until his retiremen in 1975. Mr Stevenson moved with his wife from Banbury to lodge at the Maltster an Shovell until they had a house built in 'the Backs' (later re-named Back Lane) on M Coates' land at the back of the school. They named their house Rodmarton after th place near Cirencester where Mrs Stevenson's family once lived. Mr Stevenson died i 1991 aged 76. He was a very popular man.

A class of Miss Swann's private school in July 1955 taken in her back garden. Back row, left to right: Carol? Yates, Sarah Ayers, −, −, Philip Konig, Pamela Breakspear?, −. Second row: −, −, Jeanne Yates, −, −. Third row: Geoffrey Mason, Mary Rhymes, Peter Bushnell, −. Bottom row: −, Geraldine Harris, −, Judith Smith, Alison Pegram, Caroline Searby.

Miss Helen 'Gertrude' Swann died in April 1964. A plaque in St Leonard's Church states that she was a 'friend and teacher of many Eynsham children for more than half a century.'

ountry dancing in 1949. Couples from rear to front: Shirley Leach and John Short, Margaret Gallagher and Gordon Russell, Jane Green and Roger Evans, Carol Harrison nd Kenny Brown.

Mime artist, Lindsay Kemp teaching children at Bartholomew School during his tour of Oxfordshire schools in 1967. The picture was taken by Oxford Mail photographer Johnny Johnson who lived in nearby Farmoor. (Oxford and County Newspapers)

Toad of Toad Hall was performed at Bartholomew School in December 1963. Left t right: Eric Batts (Badger), Stuart Timms (Rat) putting a hat on George Pimm (Toad Rosemary Dixey (Mole). (Oxford and County Newspapers)

# Remembering the Wars

**World War I**

Brothers George (left) and Andrew Pimm (right) both fought in the Army during World War I. Andrew was in the 55th division of the Royal Engineers and spent some of his time as a groom. When returning home from France on leave in November 1917 he travelled on a ship called the Viper.

Father and son Ernest Snr and George Harris both served their country in the same War. Ernest joined the Army Veterinary Corps when in his 40s leaving his wife and family behind to run the carrying business in Eynsham. George joined the Royal Naval Volunteer Reserve on his 18th birthday on 19 February 1918. He spent a lot of time in Cologne, Germany after the war and learnt much German using the phrase "Was ist das?".

Bert Harold Wood, a machine gunner, was killed in the First World War in 1917 and buried in Belgium. His relatives were given what was called a 'Dead Man's Penny' in his memory.

Cyril Hill's certificate of demobilisation from the Royal Air Force in 1919 havin enlisted as an 18 year old just before Armistice Day. His mother Bessie went to Franc to visit her other three sons Harvey, Jack and Nelson. Previously she had never eve been to London. The reason for her visit was that Nelson had lost a leg, and was in military hospital, and Harvey had spotted fever.

## World War II

The 2nd World War added to Eynsham's list of fatalities from war. Those from Eynsham killed were:

| | |
|---|---|
| Bayliss James Charles | Hardwick, William John |
| Booker, James | Hopkins, Thomas Henry |
| Burden, Harry Thomas | Lay, Lawrence |
| Cattell, Cecil Albert | May, Hubert |
| Christie, Malcolm Keith | Quainton, Reginald Frederick |
| Claridge, Herbert James | Snook, Alfred Arthur |
| Drew, Robert | State, Ivor William |
| Evans, Alfred William John | Walker, James |
| Green, Harry Cyril | Whelan, Graham Franklin |

Cecil Cattell, who was buried in Eynsham, was a driver in the Royal Army Service Corps killed on 8 June 1944 age 36. The Eynsham gravestone of Sapper Thomas Hopkins states that he was killed by enemy action on 16 June 1944 age 26. His brother, Signalman Walter, who was a prisoner of war in Formosa, Japan died on 15 July 1943. Private Alfred William John Evans, son of Mr and Mrs W Evans of Newland Street, of the Royal Scots Regiment, went missing on 3 April 1943 and was assumed to have died on or shortly after that date aged 31 on active service in the Middle East.

Harry Green (1923–1944)

Henry Green, known as Harry, who had been a policeman in Witney, was a lieutenant in the Oxfordshire and Buckinghamshire Light Infantry. He was found dead in northern France by a search party on 17 July 1944 shortly after his 21st birthday. He was buried nearby in Caen. Harry and those who died in the two World Wars were Eynsham's heroes who will not be forgotten.

## The Home Guard

Some of the Eynsham men in the Home Guard. Back row, left to right: — Green, —, Jock Ayres, Bill Quainton, — Lambourne, Ern? Edwards (of Cassington Road), Bill Hoskins, Walt May, Ernie? Harwood, —, Earl Green, George Bolton/— Pimm?. Front row: — Jefferies, Bert Woodhouse, (—) David Watts, —. *Lt. Wulfric Charles Freeman. O.C*

A further group of the Home Guard. Back row, left to right: Bill Harris, Don Wastie, Phil Pimm, Len Freeman, Lionel Howes, — Power, Reg Upstone, Lionel Grant?, Ted Ayers, Jack Pinker, Frank Dixey, Arthur Howard, Gordon Ayres. Front row: Bill 'Tink' Sawyer, Wallace Freeman, Perce Grant, (—) Bert Ayres, —, Walt? Bennett?.

*Lt. Wulfric Charles Freeman O.C.*

George and Rosa Green of Witney Road in their Civil Defence Volunteers uniform. The
photo was taken in June 1943

A parade of people from organisations such as the fire service and civil defence
through the Square.

## 'War Ag' (War Agricultural Executive Committee)

War Ag was a government system of increasing production on the land during and after World War II. Bitterell, off Queen Street, shown here in 1975 during the barr conversion, was the location for Eynsham's War Ag depot where agricultura equipment such as ploughs and binders was lent out. Those involved included foreman Claude Hale from Eynsham, Spence Bint from Northmoor, Tom Heslop from Churchil and Canadian Tom Richards. Tom transported goods in a big red tractor and was wel known for driving extremely fast through Eynsham.

A 1960s photograph of Claude Hale who died in 1967.

Tom Richards in 1984 with his wife Sylvia (née Merchant).

The end of the War

To celebrate the end of the war a bonfire was lit on nearby Beacon Hill. Jack Fowler, wearing a trilby, leads the way on the right-hand side with Ernie Howard leading on the left. Walter Floyd is seen behind him (wearing a cap).

Remembrance Sunday and the Eynsham branch of the Royal British Legion

Members of Eynsham's Royal British Legion leading the remembrance parade by Hall's in the 1960s. Gwen Whitlock and Mark Crawford are carrying the banners following John Nash. Ted Harris is following behind with Tommy Harris on the far left.

Cubs and Brownies were also in the procession. The man behind them talking to a man in a hat is Harold Woods. Fireman John Whitlock can also be seen with the cubs.

A team of Eynsham people cleaning the War Memorial in the Square in the 1960s. Left to right: Charlie Bowles, Bert Apsey, Christopher Betterton, Tommy Harris.

## The Falklands War

When Leonard Ayres returned to Eynsham from the Falklands the neighbours around Greens Road and Marlborough Place 'clubbed together' to buy a cup, engrave it and present it to him with a bottle of champagne. Behind Leonard, left to right: Glen Hedges, Joyce Axtell, Jackie Lewington with her child, Sandra Jones, Flossie Simpson, Mrs Chambers, Pat Burton's granddaughter and Pat, Evelyn Smith, Mrs Beach, Janet Ayres, Frances Whelan, Mrs Lacey, Barbara Allen, Temperance Hawtin, Pat Waker, Ron Gregory.

# *Eynsham Carnival*

A poster for the 1946 carnival, the first one to be held after the war.

**Bill Allsworth**

Bill as the Starter Upper at his final carnival appearance on 5 July 1997.

Bill Allsworth, who died aged 83 in 1998, was the greatly loved 'starter-upper' of the Shirt Race from its beginning in 1959 up to 1997. Bill was born in 1914, the son of Thomas Henry and Fanny Elizabeth Allsworth, in one of the cottages in Cassington Road. When about two years old the family moved further up the road to one of the cottages to the left of the White Hart. After leaving school aged 14 he worked for Dr Cruickshank earning '7 bob a week' doing various jobs such as cleaning medicine bottles and delivering letters and medicine. On reaching 16 he left to work at Lambourne being involved with the racing there. Bill then became a butler at Kingston Lyle. After his military service during World War II with time spent in Burma, Bill returned to Eynsham in 1945 and went to work at the Pressed Steel in Cowley.

Bill Allsworth, through the 'Carnival' years:

A procession outside the Shrubbery in High Street.

Bill cycling down Newland Street by the former Sawyer's shop in the 1970s.

Bill with the 1994 shirt race winners, Russell (top) and Ashley Roles (bottom), who are dressed up as Wayne and Garth, the main characters from the film 'Wayne's World.' Henry Willoughby (wearing a hat), responsible for devising the race, and Freddie Prowton, winner of the first race in 1959, are on the right.

## Jack Douglas

Jack Douglas in 1998.

Jack Douglas was born in Eynsham in 1910 and was part of the team of Scouts who started the Eynsham Carnival in 1938. Its success was repeated in 1939 with the introduction of a Carnival Queen. After the war, the British Legion then helped the Scouts with the third carnival held in 1946.

After leaving school, Jack worked as a blacksmith at Burden's in Newland Street for 14 years before spending 41 years at Hinkins & Frewin until his retirement aged 72 years. He moved away from Eynsham in 1954 following his marriage but has continued to support the carnival. The Douglas family delivered Sunday newspapers around the area for many years.

Jack was VIP in 1987 when he opened the carnival after travelling through Eynsham in the carnival parade with the then committee chairman Mike Batts, Rosie Peachey and driver Frankie Stratford.

Jack Douglas delivering his speech at the 1987 carnival. Mike Batts is to the left of the microphone.

The Eynsham Scouts celebrating the coronation of King George VI on 12 May 1937. This day's event was the inspiration for the carnival the next year. Back row, left to right: Peter Dormer, Jack Fowler, Jack Douglas, Bill Russell, Pete Blunt, –, Ron Harling, Bert Dormer, Mons Perkins, Phil Preston, Ernie Howard, Bill Perkins, Bill Bailey, Ernie Floyd, George Batts, Boss Perkins, Harry Green. Front row: Donald Good, Raymond Floyd, Chris Bryant, Bert? Whelan, Ralph Whitlock, Dennis Douglas.

'Donkey Joe'

Donkey Joe, shown above leading a pair of donkeys in the 1984 carnival, came to Eynsham in 1966 where he lived, until the last few years of his life, at St Michael's in Acre End Street. Whilst his day job was as a JCB/lorry driver for Kingston Minerals his life was devoted to animals. A great showman, many were entertained by his animals especially his donkeys that he took round at Eynsham Carnival and other events such as May Day. His donkeys, on which children loved to ride, included Rocky, No. 7, Nettle, Tay and Trigger who was actually a little Shetland pony. Joe died in 1995 aged 68.

Joe's house St Michael's in Acre End Street which backs on to Conduit Lane. The Sobranic Tobacco Company was evacuated there during World War II.

## Carnival processions, floats and getting dressed up

A procession in Station Road, probably in the pre-Carnival years.

Elsie Floyd in her carnival outfit.

A group of children in fancy dress in the mid-1950s. Left to right: Alan Pimm, Stella Holloway, Sarah Ayers, Maureen Tracy, Shenisse? Spillane. The Christmas candle behind Stella is Margaret Holloway.

A tractor pulling the carnival queen and her attendants outside Pimm's shop in the Square.

Landlord Bob Drewitt with a model of his White Hart pub in 1956.

The subject of carnival floats has been extremely varied and entertaining ranging from topical and traditional subjects to the unusual.

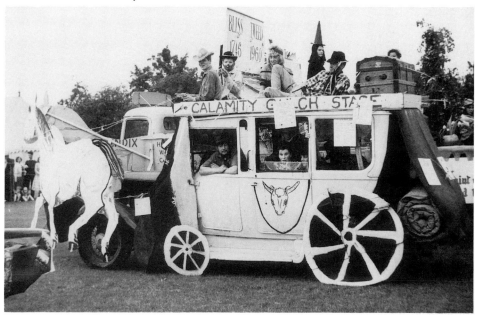

TV sitcoms have often been a topic for floats through the years. Below are Joan Reeve and Smag Ayres in the early 1960s as the characters Harold and Albert Steptoe, the well-known rag and bone men. The weather was wet that day and the colour from Joan's red braces, borrowed from Jack Thornton at the Queen's Head, ran into her shirt. The cup that the couple won can be seen on page 46.

## Carnival Queens

The first ever Carnival Queen and her attendants at the second Eynsham Carnival in 1939. Left to right: attendant Elsie Bantin, the Carnival Queen Dorothy 'Dot' Turvey (who married Bert Dormer), attendant Joan Pimm (who married Ken Harris).

Dot was presented with a bouquet of flowers by Ron Axtell. The first Carnival Queen was voted for by the school children. Ron was one of the pupils who supported Dot as a candidate. At the time of the campaign, she was in bed with tonsillitis. She was then living at Foxley Farm, run by the Hoskins family, having moved from Adderbury when she was 10. Mrs State in Acre End Street made the crown for her.

Ron and Dot in 1939 (above) and 1998 (left).

A selection of some of the Carnival Queens and their attendants over the years is shown below.

1955 Carnival Queen: Maureen Morgan. Deputy: Sheila Tibbetts. Attendants: Carole Ray and Judy Bridge

Mandy Toombs.

1969 Carnival Queen Heather McAnulla with Margie Reeves to the immediate left and Shirley Durbridge (later Gibbons) and Deborah Berry on the right.

Carnival Queen Linda Bennett.

1972 Deputy Queen Frances Smith.

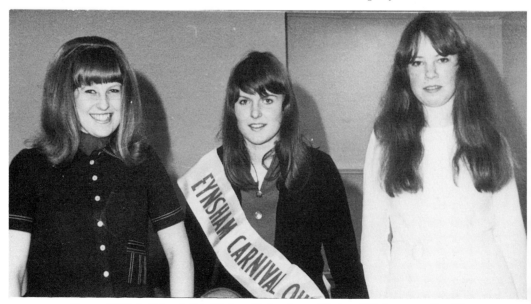

From 1970, left to right: Elaine Grimshaw, Elaine Wickson, – Smith.

## Vera Davies

It was sometime in the 1960s that Vera Davies started making the dresses for the Carnival Queens and their attendants. She has continued to do this and watches the procession, standing near the phone box in the Square and waits for the Carnival Queen float to go by with tears of emotion in her eyes.

Gladys Evans with baby Vera in Sherwood Row in 1926.

Vera's parents outside their house in Spareacre Lane in 1939.

Eynsham's popular dressmaker was born in 1926 in a cottage in Sherwood Row which led off from Mill Street where the council flats are now. Her parents were Bertie and Gladys Evans. (Another Mrs Gladys Evans was the wife of Bertie's brother Jim.) While still very young the family moved to Newland Street adjoining the house that was later the handicraft shop which was then lived in by the Blunt family. Vera's grandparents Mr and Mrs Newport also lived just along the road opposite the White Hart. Then in 1940 with younger brothers Boycott and Brian they moved to No. 8 Spareacre Lane. While at school, Vera's love of sewing developed, making chair backs with fellow pupil Barbara Howard and also dresses for teacher Mrs State. After briefly working as a machinist at Compton and Webb in Witney Vera got a job at S & N Gowns, an evacuated business from London run by Miss Siege (who lodged in Witney Road) and Russian Jew Newman Newman. The factory was in a room above the Hill brothers sawmills off the Witney Road (which has since been the site of the *Oxford Journal* and the housing estate Willows Edge). The staff consisted of one cutter, about six machinists, two pressers and two hand sewing ladies at the table. Staff remembered over the years included Rosie Peachey and her mother Mrs Herring (presser), Miss Betty State, and Hebe Treadwell from Eynsham, Winnie Smith from Hanborough, Peggie Simpson and another Winnie from Cassington, and Ruby Chambers (née Merry) from Freeland. Win Dury, briefly evacuated from London and staying with the Harrises in Farmoor, also spent a couple of months there in 1944.

In 1942 Vera met Chris Davies, a Welshman from Swansea at one of the sixpenny hops held at the Institute. He was in the RAF and based at the camp on the road to Stanton Harcourt. They married at Eynsham in 1946. Sadly Chris died in 1993.

The Evans family are so large, it is no surprise that Vera has sometimes had to make dresses on Carnival Day for her relatives. In 1997 the Carnival Queen was Adele Siret granddaughter of Pat Siret (née Evans) who is one of Vera's cousins.

Back row, left to right: Jillian Pukanuik, Adele Siret, Holly Posselwhite. Front row: Suzanne Watson, Hollie Penn, Gemma Leggett.

Vera Davies with Sylvia Ayres on an S & N Gowns outing to Bournemouth in 1947.

# *Eynsham People*

## Dr Simpson and Dr Hyde

Dr John Simpson (left) and Dr Bryan Hyde (right) at a party in January 1995 to mark their retirement from the Eynsham and Long Hanborough practices.

Dr Simpson studied medicine at Lincoln College, Oxford — where Eynsham resident and retired radiologist Dr Fred Wright had also studied. Following clinical training at the Radcliffe Infirmary and obstetrics work at Sussex Maternity Hospital, Brighton, Dr Simpson joined the practice in January 1966. He was mainly based at the surgery in Millwood End (later Churchill Way), Long Hanborough. In the 1970s he became a BMA (British Medical Association) Oxford Divisional representative. After Dr Bolsover's retirement in 1985, Dr Simpson became the senior partner. His wife, Anne, also used to summarise the patients' notes. They had two daughters — one married in nearby Hailey in 1996. Dr Simpson's hobbies include opera, reading and good food.

Dr Hyde started at the two surgeries in November 1966. He had qualified in 1961 and before Eynsham worked at various places including Bristol, Chatham, London and the 'Harley Street' of Kidderminster. He met his wife Julie, sharing a great interest in classical art, when they were both students at Cambridge. They married in 1964. They have two sons who both married in 1996.

Dr Hyde was a founding member of the Eynsham Society, Chairman of the Primary School Governors and Eynsham Play Group. He joined the Parish Council in 1972 and was chairman in 1976. (Julie was the first female chair in 1977.) Dr Hyde has also sung for the Eynsham Choral Society and played the lead in the Bartholomew Community Theatre's production of 'The Mikado'. Many other Eynsham organisations have also benefited from the Hyde family.

The site of the present Eynsham Medical Centre in Conduit Lane as it looked in early 1976. (Oxford and County Newspapers)

Although consideration had been given to using this piece of land at the rear of the then vicarage to build a church hall, the Rev Jack Westwood thought that the cost of such a hall and the benefits of a medical centre meant that it was best to sell the land to Dr Bolsover and his partners.

### Eynsham Day Centre

Once a week some of Eynsham's senior citizens attend a centre located at the rear of Bartholomew School for entertainment, lunch and, as well as other things, a good chat.

The following pictures were taken at the Day Centre in 1997.

Left to right: Vi and Bob Warren, Doris Fleet, Elsie 'Mont' Evans, Winnie Ackling.

Hilda Hollis and Alice Winterbourne.

Some of the helpers pictured in the kitchen. Left to right: Barbara Elliot, Sandra Jones (née Roberts), Anne Wrapson.

## Eynsham People

From the 1920s until the early 1980s the Harris family ran a butcher's shop on the corner of Mill Street and Acre End Street. In 1912, Fred, the only child of blacksmith Rowland Harris (whose family originated from Hailey near Witney), went to Slough to learn the butcher trade. Rowland bought the Mill Street property for his son on his marriage to Florence Mansell of Rugby. Fred and Florence had five children: Gordon, Ken, Sheila, Mervyn and John all born between the mid-1920s and mid-1930s. Nanny Lottie Floyd helped care for them.

Fred (above) was a keen horse racer and more than once won the Oxford City Plate race. A picture of his win with the horse Little Orphan appeared in the local press in August 1925. Fred was also a talented pianist.

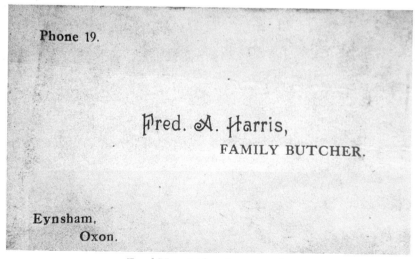

Fred Harris' business card.

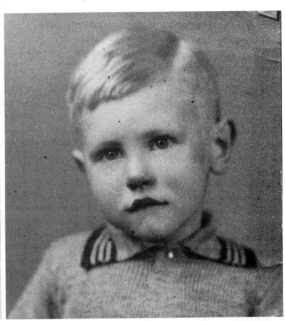

11 JUL 1934

## BEEF

| Hind Quarter. per lb. | | Fore Quarter. per lb. | |
|---|---|---|---|
| Sirloin | 1/1 | Ribs | 9 |
| Wing Rib | 1/- | Top Ribs | 9 & 10 |
| Top Side | 1/1 | Bottom Ribs | 9 & 10 |
| Silver Side | 1/1 | Thick Tops | 9 - 10 |
| Pope's Eye | 1/1 | Chuck Steak | 1/- |
| Rump | 9d | Brisket | 6 |
| Tail End Rump | 8d | Rand | 6 |
| Rump Steak | 1/6 | Beef Suet | 1/- |
| Buttock Steak | 1/3 | Shin Beef | 8d |
| Fillet Beef | 1/6 | | |
| Leg Beef | 8 | | |
| Rolled Flank | 6 | | |

| Mutton. per lb. | | Lamb. per lb. | | Pork. per lb. | |
|---|---|---|---|---|---|
| Leg | 10 | | 1/2 | Loin | 1/2 + 1/3 |
| Shoulder | 9 | | 1/- | Sparib | 1/1 |
| Loin | 8 | | 1/- | Hands | 10d |
| Best Neck | 8 | | 1/- | Cuttings | 1/3 |
| Whole " | 7 | | 9 | Streaked | & 11d |
| Scrag | 6 | | 5- | Fat | 8 |
| Breast | 3 | | 3 | Legs 1/1 cut 1/2 | |

Moore & Wingham, Printers, 39 East Street, Chichester. Tel. 283

F.A.Harris Price List 1934

Left: A 1934 price list produced by Fred Harris for Mary Oakeley when she was needing some meat for a Guides' camp.

Below: Mervyn Harris as a child.

Ken and Mervyn Harris (below) eventually took over from their father with the other sons Gordon and John running a separate butcher's shop in the Covered Market in Oxford.

Jean Buttrick (née Sawyer) is one of the best-known people in Eynsham. In the 1970s she recalled her memories of the family business in Newland Street by writing *Our Shop*. This led to her being a very popular speaker for organisations such as the Women's Institute in the Oxfordshire area. Her sister Ann also lives in Eynsham.

A very early picture, from the turn of the century, of Sawyer's shop. Note the shoes, bed posts and bath tubs outside the building.

.nother early photograph of Sawyer's shop. On the right can be seen the adjoining
ork butcher's shop of the Hirons family.

# W. SAWYER & SONS,

## Grocers & Provision Merchants,

### Ironmongers & Cycle Agents,

BEDDING AND FURNITURE WAREHOUSE,
◡DRAPERS & GENERAL OUTFITTERS.
DEALERS IN CHINA, GLASS AND EARTHENWARE,

Patent Medicine Vendors,

SEEDSMEN, NEWSVENDORS & STATIONERS,

Agent for the " Sun " Fire and Life, and " Scottish Accident " Insurance Companies.

***

## EYNSHAM STORES, OXON.

he Sawyers' family business card. (See also Book 1, page 63 for pictures of the shop in
ter years.)

Jean Buttrick's and Ann Haines' father, Bill 'Tink' Sawyer, in the 1920s with his motorbike and sidecar. The dog is a whippet by the name of Sailor Boy. Tink kept greyhounds in kennels in his garden behind the shop (known as Sawyer's back). He used them for racing at places like Oxford Stadium and Swindon.

Phillis Harris shown here in the early latter half of the 1930s wearing a blouse that was made by Dot Aldridge.

he house where Dorothy 'Dot' Aldridge's handicraft shop was. Following Major
akeley's death, the Oakeleys moved into this house and Dot moved to 4 Wytham View
here she lived until her death aged 90 years in March 1980. She was known for being
ne of the kindest and most thoughtful people in Eynsham.

Miss Dot Aldridge as a young adult.

Steve Flynn, one of Dot's evacuees and
Alan Wooldridge in Wytham View.

Steve came from the dock area of Poplar, London although by the end of the war his
other had moved to Nelson in Lancashire. It was there, by the age of 19 he was one of
ngland's youngest cinema managers.

Dot Aldridge's Village Handicraft shop is advertised in this 1929 Eynsham Parish Magazine.

Mary Oakeley, who died in December 1997 aged 84, just a few weeks after having her autobiography published, achieved a great deal in her life. As a young child, she was taught in Eynsham by Miss Swann. She later studied at St Hilda's College, Oxford, having cycled from Eynsham to the interview. After starting her teaching career at St James' School in West Malvern, Mary went on to become a headmistress at the young age of 26 in a school in Timaru, New Zealand. Following her retirement, she was of great support to the sick and needy in Eynsham. She was greatly involved in St Leonard's church and was the second woman in the Anglican church to be made a lay reader. All her talents gave her an entry in *Who's Who.*

Left to right: June Harris, Eileen Crampton, Mary Oakeley.

Jess Treadwell worked as a milkman for Franklins Farm at Swinford. He is shown here delivering milk in Mill Street near where the Options hairdressing shop now is. One of the late Harold Quainton's first jobs on leaving school was assisting Jess.

Lottie Pimm (1904–1994) worked in the family shop in the Square, taught children Morris dancing and helped with the Red Cross during World War II. Until her death she lived at Llandaff in the Square.

Members of the Howard family with friends in the Star in the 1950s. Back row, left to right: Arthur Howard Snr, Ron Lee, Arthur Howard Jnr, –, 'Babe' Axtell, Mike Howard. Front row: Roy Howard, Aubrey Howard, Elsie Howard, Ron Axtell, Jim Grimshaw (landlord).

The above photograph was taken by war veteran and former Japanese prisoner of war Arthur Titherington. Arthur used to be based at 25 Wytham View. The former Witney mayor now has a photographic studio in Church Green, Witney.

Girls celebrating May Day in the Square in 1952. Left to right: Pauline Pimm, Barbara Brown, Veronica Bailey, Judy Bridges, Jackie McCuddon, Carol Bernard, Janet Hailey, Beryl Gallagher, Rita Wixey.

A group of ladies in the 1960s who were taking a break from potato picking. Left to right: Hilda Gallagher, Violet Warren, Veronica 'Ron' Simpson, –.

The Women's Institute in the mid-1930s on a trip out. Front row, left to right: 1 Elsie Green, 2 Miss Mabel Betterton with nephew 3 Derek Parker, 4 Rosa Green and son 5 Bill, 6 Barbara Hill and mother 7 Ida Hill, 8 Gwen Whitlock, 9 Eva Green (wife of Brandy), 10 Natalie Belcher. Second row: 1 Alice Parker (née Betterton), 2 – Dixey (grandmother of Bill Green)?, 3 Lottie Hedges?, 4 Eva Howard, 5 Maud Hill, 6 –, 7 –, 8 Mrs Dormer, 9 Mrs Dixey (mother of Raymond), 10 Mrs Calcutt (mother of Cecil). The back rows: 1 Miss Helens (of Home Farm Cottage, Mill St), 2 Mrs Rusher, 3 Mrs Watts of City Farm, 4 Mrs Batts, 5 –, 6 –, 7 Mrs Watkins?, 8 Mrs Mayne of Toner House, 9 –, 10 Mrs Holliday of Mill St, 11 –, 12 Mrs Wilkins, 13 sister of 15?, 14 –, 15 Hilda Brooks?, 16 Mrs Farnish, 17 Miss Hopkins' sister, 18 Kitty Howard. The WI celebrated its 75th anniversary in 1998.